NO
THANKS

TO
Farrar & Rinehart
Simon & Schuster
Coward-McCann
Limited Editions
Harcourt, Brace
Random House
Equinox Press
Smith & Haas
Viking Press
Knopf
Dutton
Harper's
Scribner's
Covici-Friede

THE CUMMINGS TYPESCRIPT EDITIONS

This series of the published and unpublished writings of E. E. Cummings is based upon the author's typed and autographed manuscripts in The Houghton Library, Harvard University; the Clifton Waller Barrett Library, University of Virginia; The University of Texas Humanities Research Center; and The Beinecke Rare Book and Manuscript Library, Yale University. The cooperation and assistance of these institutions and their librarians, curators, and staffs are hereby gratefully acknowledged.

It is the aim of The Cummings Typescript Editions to present the texts of the poet's works exactly as he created them, in versions that are faithful to the letter as well as the spirit of his originals. This does not present any difficulties with reference to his plays, essays, letters, and narrative prose. However, as Cummings himself observed, it is impossible "to retranslate [his] poems [and poetic prose] out of typewriter language into linotype-ese" without distorting the spatial values of the works themselves. The "typewriter language" of the poems and poetic prose has therefore been retained. These works have been prepared for publication by George James Firmage, the editor of the series.

E E Cummings

NO THANKS

Edited, with an Afterword, by
George James Firmage

Introduction by
Richard S. Kennedy

Liveright
NEW YORK

FIRST EDITION

Published simultaneously in Canada
by George J. McLeod Limited, Toronto

Library of Congress Cataloging in Publication Data

Cummings, Edward Estlin, 1894–1962.
  No thanks.
  I. Firmage, George James. II. Title.
PS3505.U334N6 1978   811'.5'2   78–3827
ISBN 0–87140–631–4
ISBN 0–87140–120–7 pbk.

This book was designed by John Harmer.
Typefaces used are IBM Delegate,
Baskerville and Rockwell Light.
Printing and binding were done by The Murray Printing Co.

PRINTED IN THE UNITED STATES OF AMERICA
1 2 3 4 5 6 7 8 9 0

INTRODUCTION

by

Richard S. Kennedy

I

Although E. E. Cummings's *No Thanks* was published in 1935 in the middle of his career, the story of its appearance indicates that he was still far from achieving recognition as an important American writer. The whole venture began well enough, for he received a Guggenheim fellowship in 1933 to carry out a project that he described on the application form in four words, "a book of poems" (surely, the briefest description of a project that the Guggenheim Foundation ever received). But the following year, when he sought a publisher for the book of poems he had produced, he could find no taker, even though in the previous dozen years he had published five volumes of poetry, a play, a collection of his art works, and two remarkable prose narratives, one of which, *The Enormous Room,* had continued to be reprinted since 1922.

If we look more closely at the situation, we can understand some of the difficulties. In the mid-1930s American publishers were floundering in the slough of the Great Depression and Cummings's unusual creations held no attraction for them. Liveright, who had published Cummings's two previous volumes of poetry, was having no luck at all in the market with them. In the first six months of 1935, the company sold only thirteen copies of *Is 5* and two copies of *ViVa.* Covici-Friede, the firm that published Cummings's *Eimi,* his most important prose work, had sold exactly one copy during the last half of 1934. After sending his manuscript around for several months without success, Cummings gave up. He was only able to get the book in print when his mother put up a three-hundred-dollar subsidy for private publication at the Golden Eagle Press. The declaration of "No Thanks" which Cummings placed at the beginning of the book lists the publishers who turned him down—their names arranged carefully to form the shape of a funeral urn.

Another problem was the make-up of the collection of poems itself. *No Thanks* contains more linguistic experiments and more obscurities than any volume Cummings ever produced. He was always uncritical about his published work and ready to include jokes, ephemeral epigrams, and private poems along with memorable lyrics and technically brilliant linguistic compositions. Since in this collection the doubtful items are found in the first half of the book, this placement in itself must have helped to discourage editors. Thus we can be grateful that the book got into print at all, so that we can now stand back from the work to see it as a whole, before we make discriminations among individual poems.

When we do, we can become aware of two distinct aspects of *No Thanks:* the pattern in which the poems are arranged and the highly individual view of life that the totality of the work reveals. Here, as in his other books, Cummings consciously strove to put his materials in a carefully planned order. When he first assembled his poems for publication, he arranged them in a "schema" (he learned the term in his Dante course at Harvard) which he thought of in the shape of a caret. Starting with a piece about "snow," he set up a pattern of three poems followed by a sonnet, then three more poems and another sonnet, and so on up to "poem 35," again a "snow" poem; then a peak of three sonnets; then descending on the other side he began with "poem 39," which had "star" as its subject, and again the pattern of three poems followed each time by a sonnet, until the end, "Sonnet XIX," another "star" poem.[1] Here are the notes showing his design:

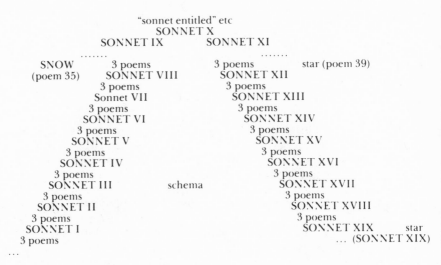

"sonnet entitled" etc
SONNET X
SONNET IX   SONNET XI

SNOW   3 poems   3 poems   star (poem 39)
(poem 35)   SONNET VIII   SONNET XII
3 poems   3 poems
Sonnet VII   SONNET XIII
3 poems   3 poems
SONNET VI   SONNET XIV
3 poems   3 poems
SONNET V   SONNET XV
3 poems   3 poems
SONNET IV   SONNET XVI
3 poems   3 poems
SONNET III   schema   SONNET XVII
3 poems   3 poems
SONNET II   SONNET XVIII
3 poems   3 poems
SONNET I   SONNET XIX   star
3 poems   ... (SONNET XIX)

snow   ...
(poem 1)

Revision and reworking brought about the final schema which governs the book. Cummings visualized it in the shape of a V: the movement from two "moon" poems, descending to "earth" poems at the center of the book, and then rising to two "star" poems at the conclusion.

°2 moons   *2 stars
('mOOn Over tOwns mOOn')   ('brIght')
('moon over gai')   ('morsel miraculous and meaningless')
NO THANKS:schema of construction

°2 poems   2 poems*
sonnet I   sonnet XVIII
3 poems   3 poems
sonnet II   sonnet XVII
3 poems   3 poems
sonnet III   sonnet XVI
3 poems   3 poems
sonnet IV   sonnet XV
3 poems   3 poems
sonnet V   sonnet XIV
3 poems   3 poems
sonnet VI   sonnet XIII
3 poems   3 poems
sonnet VII   sonnet XII
3 poems   3 poems
sonnet VIII   sonnet XI
3 poems   3 poems
('how dark and single,where—sonnet IX   sonnet X—('conceive a man,should he
he ends,the earth')   1 poem   have anything')[2]
('into a truly')

The other distinctive feature of the book is the presence of Cummings's view of life—romantic individualism—here revealed in its extremes. To begin with, Cummings held that the essential self of any human being was an instinctive complex of consciousness which responded harmoniously to the world by "feeling"; hence, he regarded mind and its analytical powers as only a suppressant, and he considered intellectual systems (usually referred to as "science") to be the enemy of happiness for the instinctive self. Whatever the instinctive self desires to express is good: one should follow impulse; one should thrust aside caution or restraint. He saw the population of the world as a multifarious mixture of unique selves, each of whom can achieve the good life if he freely acts out his uniqueness and avoids the pressures imposed by society to behave otherwise. This is an optimistic view, too, because Cummings considered that the essential self is in its tendencies good and loving and that it would only become twisted into evil by outside forces. Socially and politically this is an anarchistic view, for society in general and government in particular are seen to be always attempting to curb the activities of the individual.

The poems begin to exhibit these views negatively. Poem 7, "sonnet entitled how to run the world" gives a succinct answer, "don't." (Note that in the first schema, Cummings had placed this poem at the apex of his caret.) Poem 23 invites us to observe a man who "does not have to feel because he thinks," and if that is not bad enough for him, the thoughts are supplied by other people. Certainty is even worse: "he does not have to think because he knows." Thus Life (reverently capitalized) looks down upon one whose natural emotional existence is crushed, making him one of the living dead. American life, it is implied, is especially repressive because of its demands for conformity. Again and again in other poems, Cummings hoots at pretentions to "progress" which overvalue technological achievement and at advertising ballyhoo which promotes the commercialization of modern culture. These are forces that encourage the standardization of human life. But he reserves his greatest scorn for the totalitarian state which makes complete and willing slaves out of its "kumrads."

More positively, the poems will be seen to celebrate an openly felt response to the beauties of the natural world—stars, snow, birds, flowers, and even such minor miracles as grasshoppers or mice. The poems optimistically express joy in the time of beginnings, spring, and they give first place to love among all the feelings—love in all of its manifestations, especially in fully shared sexual intercourse.

These attitudes give rise to a special evaluative vocabulary, to which Cummings sometimes gives additional emphasis when he alters normal grammatical usages—that is, when he uses verbs as nouns, adverbs as adjectives, and so on. "Alive" is one of the chief value terms, and the verb "is," the essence of being alive, will be isolated for special veneration (for example, the "isful" star in the last line of the book, or the affirmative declaration in poem 67 that "Is will still occur" in spite of the threats of "knowings" and their "credos"). "Guess" is one of the good words, along with "dare," "open," "dream," and "yes"; "reason" is a bad one, as well as "same," "shut," "numb," and "most(people" or "most)people." When Cummings is speaking of people, the good relative pronoun is "who" because it refers to human beings; the bad one is "which" because it refers to things.

When we see that the poems in an accumulative way express a totality of outlook, we are then less inclined to regret Cummings's lack of taste when he includes something on the level of a college humor magazine like poem 16, "may i feel said he," or his self-indulgence when he includes a private poem like poem 27, a hexameter sonnet in praise of his friend Joseph Gould, a Harvard graduate who eschewed possessions and became a beggar in Greenwich Village and thus the ultimate urban romantic. Also, if to dare is good, then to play around in poem 20 with the Biblical quotation "Go to the ant, thou sluggard; consider her ways be wise" can be acceptable, even though the poem comes to an abrupt anticlimax. Or we can put up with the cheap shots directed at the Chicago World's Fair (its theme was "A Century of Progress") in poem 42, if we see that they are consistent with his general scheme of values: the fleshly reality of Sally Rand's fan dance is to be preferred above the mechanical quality of phonograph music ("croons canned à la vallee") and the artificial life of moving pictures ("preserved goldfishian gestures").[3]

When we begin to examine poetic experiment and linguistic play, we are considering aspects of Cummings's technique that go beyond the question of whether or not certain ideas or attitudes are worthy of poetic expression, and we are reminded that his manipulation of language may provide aesthetic pleasure no matter what kind of material he is treating and that nothing can be considered as "not a proper subject for poetry." A case in point is poem 9, which satirizes the custom that the president of the United States will throw out the first baseball of the season. Cummings's ingenious spatial handling brings aesthetic life to this unpromising subject. Cummings pitches an initial "o" past a whole team of eleven lines before we realize that it has the roundness of a baseball. It is then picked up, after we have forgotten it, to be used again for "supposedly" and "throwing." The spacing, both horizontal and vertical, toward the end of the poem is appropriately representative of the throwing down of the ball, and the letters that Cummings has isolated to show its fall can be seen, after a moment's look, to divide into "win" and "gab," two words which are part of the season's activity. The accumulative repetition of words "The/(The president The/president of The president/of the…," and so on, mounts like fanfare preceding the president's act, and the Latin words which Cummings then supplies "unde negant redire quemquam" (hence denying anyone to say again) adds to the factitious pomp.

Years earlier when Cummings was first developing his unusual poetic practice which involved spatial arrangements as well as typographical and linguistic play, he thought of doing away with the word "poem" and substituting *"fait,"* a French term for "the thing made," and he thought of himself as a *faiteur.* It is regrettable that he did not act upon his idea, for the terminology is wonderfully suitable to some of the work we find in *No Thanks.* The grasshopper poem, number 13, is a brilliant instance. In this linguistic construct everything depends on devices that are in no way associated with traditional poetry.

These untraditional works (no one would ever call them verses) frequently exhibit a burst of genuine creative joy in the use of language. Poem 40, "as if as," presents a complex developing action. At base, it is the description of a foggy dawn. But as the description of the gradual coming of light and the rising sun proceeds, we are gradually aware that a birth is suggested, too, by means of the elements which are introduced: the phrase "i am alive," the cry, and the compressed word "budofshape." Finally, when the sunrise is linguistically forcing its way upward in the final line,

mmamakmakemakesWwOwoRworLworlD

we note that Cummings has provided for the presence of the word "mama" so that we can understand that mama makes world, too, in this *fait* which is about coming into being.

Cummings cared deeply about form, and if these poems themselves did not tell us, then his arrangement of the whole collection insists on it, for he has placed at the very center of his seventy-one poems (flanked on either side by a sonnet) a poem about creating:

> into a truly
> curving form
> enters my
> soul

in which the creative experience is likened to a terrifying ancient-marinerlike voyage. The ship (as form) makes its way through a chaos of night and nonbeing, and the poem ends with the verb that is most significant in the Cummings lexicon:

> whose passenger and whose
> pilot my spirit is

Cummings is sometimes criticized for writing a great many of the same kinds of poems. But it would be more just to say this: that his stylistic manner is distinctive and he does not abandon it—anymore than Whitman or Hopkins abandon theirs. And like those distinctive stylists, he maintains his view of life consistently as he continues to develop features of his unique way of saying things. It is actually difficult in a limited space to make an adequate commentary on the variety of his poems. But to take a quick glance for illustration, we can note poems 57, 58, 59, and 60. Within four pages we have (a) a sonnet about a hand organ playing in springtime as two lovers join together in the wonder of "IYou"; (b) two brief, delicately balanced stanzas celebrating love and affirming life as forms of unity that embrace multiplicity; (c) a visually directive poem, descriptive of a bright spring Sunday morning resounding with church bells; and (d) a poem of developing action in which language, typography, and punctuation combine to present a striptease artist and in which occur verse paragraphs like this:

> unununun?
> butbutbut??
> tonton???
> ing????

(It plays with a single word and a single punctuation mark but manages to convey a multitude of meanings: the beginning of a divestiture and a French word suggesting a single something; a hesitation and the possibility of a change of mind; the French word for "your" and thus a shift to giving; and a sense of progression—all this in a pattern of diminishing substance and, through punctuation, of increasing mystery.)

Before leaving these introductory considerations, we should look at the two "star" poems which conclude the book, for they represent something new in Cummings's poetry—a religious tone. Earlier in *No Thanks,* his ballade, poem 54, had begun its envoi with the lines "King Christ, this world is all aleak;/and lifepreservers there are none," but the Christ reference here, I think, is only an echo of the François Villon tradition, for that medieval maker of ballades also called upon "Prince Christ" in his envois. Cummings was not a Christian. His father, the Reverend Edward Cummings, had brought up his son Estlin in the beliefs of that halfway station, the Unitarian Church, which regards Christ not as God but as a holy man who brought a special message about worshiping God and living the moral life. Yet for twenty years now, Estlin had professed none of the beliefs of Boston Unitarianism. By 1934, however, he had been through a lot of anguish and the heartbreak of two divorces, and when he met his third wife Marion Morehouse, who was a Roman Catholic, he was more open to the religious views which she still retained, although she herself was not active in her religion. Years before, Estlin Cummings had rebelled vigorously against his father and much of what he stood for, but now almost ten years had passed since Edward Cummings's death and Estlin had been moving gradually toward a reconciliation with what he had rejected.

All this is by way of background to the "star" poems. For whatever reasons—the influence of Marion Morehouse, a gesture toward the memory of his father, or an extension of his own sense of cosmic order—these star poems introduce a new note into Cummings's book of poems. They suggest the Reverend Edward Cummings's "religion of the star" as he called it. To sum up the matter very briefly: Edward Cummings disliked the Christian emphasis on the crucifixion as the central event in the Christian theology, because of the stress on sin and suffering. He preferred a religion of joy and brotherly love, and he selected the star of Bethlehem rather than the cross as his principal religious symbol. To him it signified not only a joyful sense of newness in a rebirth of the world but also the light that shone down on all humankind, rich and poor, in all the nations of the earth, and the angels' song of "peace and good will to men" was for him the message of "the religion of the star."[4]

A few words and phrases like "holy," "miraculous," "lifting hopes and hands" and an attitude of wonder and humility before some higher otherness add the religious coloration to the star poems. The final one is a syntactical scramble, too complex for explication here.[5] But a brief comment on the penultimate poem seems necessary in order to call attention to some features which make this one of Cummings's most pleasingly patterned linguistic experiments. As Robert McIlvaine has pointed out, there are only eleven discrete words used in the fifteen-line poem, but they are deployed in such a way that they make up a total of forty-four words: the three-letter words "big," "yes," and "who" are used three times; the four-letter words "soft," "near," "calm," "holy," "deep," and "star," four times; the five-letter word "alone," five times; the six-letter word "bright," six times.[6] There is no English sentence at all—only a construct of words. But a statement emerges by means of patterns.

The lines are arranged in a numerical progression from the first line, standing alone, to a five-line final group. Another progression moves from "s???" to the full spelling of "star," as if the star gradually comes into being. "Bright" orthographically disappears into "?????T," as if dawn comes isolating the morning star and then causes it to fade out. Suggestion builds into meaning that this is a poem about the star of Bethlehem, a meaning greatly aided by the conjunction of words like "bright," "holy," and "calm" in their allusion to the Christmas hymn "Silent night, holy night./All is calm, all is bright." The pattern of capital letters at length spells out BRIGHT, YES, and WHO and is completed with the last line when the capital "Who" remains "(holy alone) holy (alone holy) alone." Edward Cummings would have been gratified.

Cummings placed his dedication to his mother, "AND THANKS TO R.H.C.," at the end of the book. It is appropriate in its place next to the star poems, memorials of her husband's religious symbols. Her money was well spent.

Temple University
March 1978

Notes

[1]Houghton Library, Harvard University, bMS AM1823.7 (22), folder 7. I wish to record here my special thanks to Ms. Marte Shaw, curator of the Houghton Library Reading Room, and her staff for their courtesy and help.

[2]George Firmage discovered this manuscript in the Clifton Waller Barrett Library, University of Virginia, Deposit 6246-a.

[3]Cummings usually referred to Samuel Goldwyn of Metro-Goldwyn-Mayer Studio by his earlier name, Samuel Goldfish.

[4]For a full discussion of Edward Cummings's theology, see my article "Edward Cummings, the Father of the Poet," *Bulletin of the New York Public Library,* 70 (September 1966), 437–449.

[5]For a full explication, see Valarie Arms, "A Catholic Reading of Cummings' 'morsel miraculous and meaningless,'" *Journal of Modern Literature* (April 1978).

[6]Robert McIlvaine, "Cummings' 'Bright,'" *Explicator,* 30 (September 1971), 6.

NO
THANKS

mOOn Over tOwns mOOn
whisper
less creature huge grO
pingness

whO perfectly whO
flOat
newly alOne is
dreamest

oNLY THE MooN o
VER ToWNS
SLoWLY SPRoUTING SPIR
IT

moon over gai
-té.a
sharp crone dodders be-
tween taxis swirl hues crowds mov
-ing ing ing
among who dreams whom mutterings dream &

:the moon over death over edgar the
moon
      over smellings of gently smell of deads
(lovers grip sprawl twitch lovers)
& one dog?piglike big!sorrows

always;finally and always,the iflike moon over moving
me—the
moon
m
ov—in
g
over(moving)you beautifully also;at

denfert the fat strongman has put
down his carpet from which rise slim curving mighty
children while a python over the way freezes
a serpent becomes a
rod smiles
the liontamer nearby hieroglyphs
soar dip
dip
soar equalling noise solemn

dolls re
-volve whirlswans rabbitsare:
swimswim
painted-with-horses-with-painted-
with eyes and the.m

oon over juillet moon over s
-unday

O:
m
o
o
n
o
  (ver no(w ove(r all;
                o
ver pinkthisgreen acr)o)greenthatpink)
acrobata

mong
trees climbing on
A

pi llarofch airso vertheseu pstareth oseings
over
(a hard a
hard a girl a girl)sing
-ing ing(ing
sing)ing a soft a song a softishsongly
v
 o
  i
   c
    e o
       ver
(whi!tethatr?apidly
legthelessne sssuc kedt oward
black,this

)roUnd ingrOundIngly rouNdar(round)ounDing
                              ;ball
                               balll
                               ballll
                               balllll

that which we who're alive in spite of mirrors
(have died beyond the clock)we,of ourselves

who more a part are(less who are aware)

than of my books could even be your shelves
(that which we die for;not when or unless
if or to prove,imperfectly or since

but through spontaneous deft strictly horrors

which stars may not observe;while roses wince)
that which we die for lives(may never cease
views with smooth vigilant perpetual eyes
each exact victim,how he does not stir)

0 love,my love!soul clings and heart conceives

and mind leaps(and that which we die for lives
as wholly as that which we live for dies)

i
(meet)t(touch)
ems crouch(
)ing bruiseD
Suddenly by thousand

starings rinsed with
thoroughly million yells they
f-oo-1(whom,blinds;blood)pa-nt
stab are

(slopped givers of not)bang
spurting mesh(faith
-ful which -ly try are ing)al

most fe(hug)males(one-t
wo-1 oop-1

eftsthrowr ightsm issingupperc

uts-1urc hhurt-re
coil charge &)swooN

Crowdloomroar:ing;diskface,es
(are two
notSoft soft one are

hard one notHard)not
boys boy-
ish(a stopped A)with!notgirl'swith?dumb
(thewith girl)ness(ish The eyesthe

Is)aRe
iS ar(ise)wi
lt(wit(hprettyw)ith)mr
jeff dick
son fec

i
(m
c)
t

(m
x
x

x
ii)

I

a)glazed mind layed in a
                              urinal
howlessly and without why
(quite minus gal or
                    pal

slightly too sick to rightly die)
"gedup"
        the gentscoon coos
gently:tug?g(ing intently it

refuses.
        to refuse;
just,look)ing dead but not complete
-ly not(not as look men

who are turned to seem)
                        "stetti"
and
    willbeishfully bursting un-
eats wasvino isspaghett(i

exit a kind of unkindness exit

little
mr Big
notbusy
Busi
ness notman

(!ye
galleon
wilts
b:
  e;n,d

i
 ng
like like,like bad,like
candy:& you

are dead
you captain)

Memo 1
wife in impossibly
hell Memo
1 son
in improbably yale

sonnet entitled how to run the world)

A always don't there B being no such thing
for C can't casts no shadow D drink and

E eat of her voice in whose silence the music of spring
lives F feel opens but shuts understand
G gladly forget little having less

with every least each most remembering
H highest fly only the flag that's furled

(sestet entitled grass is flesh or swim
who can and bathe who must or any dream
means more than sleep as more than know means guess)

I item i immaculately owe
dying one life and will my rest to these

children building this rainman out of snow

the(
    Wistfully

dead seem generous)don't
All suspect each(nor

have i observed
some chucking some
legally into Oblivion wave little

flags weeping flatter
thoroughly imploring threaten)the
wistFully dead you directly perceive or minus
news alimony blackmail whathavewe

and propaganda(it is incredible But
others don't
scream murmur wink
at kid anaesthetize marry bump off
or otherwise amplify others)

the so to speak wistfully dead
are not relatively
speaking uncultured(who
Very distinctly confine

their omnipotent literally their
putting it more than mildly Absolute
destructivity to non-

entities e.
g. the)
    whis-per it
           (

Living

o pr
gress verily thou art m
mentous superc
lossal hyperpr
digious etc i kn
w & if you d

n't why g
 to yonder s
called newsreel s
called theatre & with your
wn eyes beh

ld The
         (The president The
         president of The president
         of the The)president of

         the(united The president of the
         united states The president of the united
         states of The President Of The)United States

         Of America unde negant redire quemquam supp
sedly thr

w
 i
  n
   g
    a
     b
       aseball

```
little man
(in a hurry
full or an
important worry)
halt stop forget relax

wait

(little child
who have tried
who have failed
who have cried)
lie bravely down

sleep

big rain
big snow
big sun
big moon
(enter

us)
```

ci-gît 1 Foetus(unborn to not die

safely whose epoch fits him like a grave)
with all his toys(money men motors "my"
yachts wolfhounds women)and the will to shave

that Ghost is dead(whom noone might inter)
fleeing himself for selves more strangely made
(wears pain at joy,come summer puts on fur

answers eats moves remembers is afraid)

each hates a Man whom both would call their friend
and who may envy neither;nor bewail
(would rather make than have and give than lend
—being through failures born who cannot fail)

having no wealth but love,who shall not spend
my fortune(although endlessness should end)

why why

How many winds make wonderful
and is luck The skeleton of life
or did anybody Open a moment

are Not

more than(if Green invents because
where might Where live
can fisherMen swim and
who's myself's Antimere
Should words carry weapons)'are

not Less than(that

by doDreaming heteronomously
metameric me are picked from
dumb sleePdeep
ness squirmcurl

ing homonomously metameric You

                              r-p-o-p-h-e-s-s-a-g-r
                    who
a)s w(e loo)k
upnowgath
          PPEGORHRASS
                          eringint(o-
aThe):l
        eA
            !p:
S   a
                      (r
  rIvInG   .gRrEaPsPhOs)
                                                    to
  rea(be)rran(com)gi(e)ngly
  ,grasshopper;

mouse)Won
derfully is
anyone else entirely who doesn't
move(Moved more suddenly than)whose

tiniest smile?may Be
bigger than the fear of all
hearts never which have
(Per

haps)loved(or than
everyone that will Ever love)we
've
hidden him in A leaf

and,
Opening
beautiful earth
put(only)a Leaf among dark

ness.sunlight's
thenlike?now
Disappears
some

thing(silent:
madeofimagination
;the incredible soft)ness
(his ears(eyes

to rearrangingly become

one nonsufficiently inunderstood
re
   with some difficulty
                    one father of
one(ask super-)wonderful(mother)child is a good
Husband to him(and whose what he conceives to be Love
did
     stretchandstretchandstretchandstretchand
                            did)
who begins stuttering each sentence we both
consid
     (notb- notbr- notbre- notbrea-k
                        The kid)
er Santa Claus a criminal(hears Darwin;asks about Death)
concept

     O hairlesschested females,well
attend!list,every nonelastic male—
uplook,all joybegotten whelps whom soothe
psychotic myths like Jonah And The Whale

:oiwun uhsoi roitee runow dutmoi
jak roids wid yooze
           Vury Sin Silly
                  :oi

may i feel said he
(i'll squeal said she
just once said he)
it's fun said she

(may i touch said he
how much said she
a lot said he)
why not said she

(let's go said he
not too far said she
what's too far said he
where you are said she)

may i stay said he
(which way said she
like this said he
if you kiss said she

may i move said he
is it love said she)
if you're willing said he
(but you're killing said she

but it's life said he
but your wife said she
now said he)
ow said she

(tiptop said he
don't stop said she
oh no said he)
go slow said she

(cccome?said he
ummm said she)
you're divine!said he
(you are Mine said she)

o
sure)but
nobody unders(no
but Rully yes i
know)but what it comes

to(listen you don't have to

i mean Reely)but(no listen don't
be sil why sure)i mean the(o
well ughhuh sure why not yuh course yeh well
naturally i und certain i o posi but

i know sure that's)but listen here's

(correct you said it yeah)but
listen but(it's Rilly yeh
ughhuh yuh)i know

(o sure i

know yes
of

course)but what i mean is Nobody Understands Her RERLY

this little
pair had a little scare
right in the middle of a bed bed
bed)when each other courted both
was very very thwarted(and
when which was aborted
what was dead dead dead)

whereupon mary
quite contrary didn't
die
(may be seen to inexactly pass and unprecisely
to repass where
flesh is heiry montparnasse
is goosed by raspail).

But he turned into a fair
y!a fair
y!!a
fair
y!!!
but she turned into a fair-y(and
it seems to be doing nicely

who before dying demands not rebirth

of such than hungrily more swiftness as
with(feel)pauseless immeasurably Now
cancels the childfully diminishing earth
—never whose proudly life swallowed is by

(with hope two eyes a memory this brow
five or three dreamfuls of despair that face)

large onecoloured nonthings of gluttonous sky—
nor(as a blind,how timidly,throb;which
hints being;suggests identity)breathes fleet
perfectly far from tangible domains
rare with most early soul
                              him shall untouch

meaningless precision and complete fate

(he must deny mind:may believe in brains.

go(perpe)go

(tu)to(al
adve

nturin
g p
article

s of s
ini
sterd
exte

ri)go to(ty)the(om
nivorou salways lugbrin
g ingseekfindlosin g
motilities
are)go to

the
ant
(al
ways

alingwaysing)
go to the ant thou go
(inging)

to the
ant,thou ant-

eater

21

IN)
    all those who got
    athlete's mouth jumping
    on&off bandwaggons
                (MEMORIAM

when muckers pimps and tratesmen
delivered are of vicians
and all the world howls stadesmen
beware of politisions

beware of folks with missians
to turn us into rissions
and blokes with ammunicions
who tend to make incitions

and pity the fool who cright
god help me it aint no ews
eye like the steak all ried
but eye certainly hate the juse

he does not have to feel because he thinks
(the thoughts of others,be it understood)
he does not have to think because he knows
(that anything is bad which you think good)

because he knows,he cannot understand
(why Jones don't pay me what he knows he owes)
because he cannot understand,he drinks
(and he drinks and he drinks and he drinks and)

not bald.   (Coughs.)   Two pale slippery small eyes

balanced upon one broken babypout
(pretty teeth wander into which and out
of)Live,dost Thou contain a marvel than
this death named Smith less strange?
                              Married and lies

afraid; aggressive and:American

"let's start a magazine

to hell with literature
we want something redblooded

lousy with pure
reeking with stark
and fearlessly obscene

but really clean
get what I mean
let's not spoil it
let's make it serious

something authentic and delirious
you know something genuine like a mark
in a toilet

graced with guts and gutted
with grace"

squeeze your nuts and open your face

this(that

grey)white
(man)horse

floats
on 4
3rdtoes

p
(drooli
ngly supp
ort 2 be

nt
toothpick
s)

ro
ude

stly(stuck in a spanked behind

what does little Ernest croon
in his death at afternoon?
(kow dow r 2 bul retoinis
wus de woids uf lil Oinis

little joe gould has lost his teeth and doesn't know where
to find them(and found a secondhand set which click)little
gould used to amputate his appetite with bad brittle
candy but just(nude eel)now little joe lives on air

Harvard Brevis Est for Handkerchief read Papernapkin no laundry
bills likes People preferring Negroes Indians Youse
n.b. ye twang of little joe(yankee)gould irketh sundry
who are trying to find their minds(but never had any to lose)

and a myth is as good as a smile but little joe gould's quote oral
history unquote might(publishers note)be entitled a wraith's
progress or mainly swash while chiefly submerged or an amoral
morality sort-of-aliveing by innumerable kind-of-deaths

(Amérique Je T'Aime and it may be fun to be fooled
but it's more fun to be more to be fun to be little joe gould)

that famous fatheads find that each
    and every thing must have an end
(the silly cause of trivial which
    thinkless unwishing doth depend

    upon the texture of their p-ss)
isn't(and that it mayn't be twirled
    around your little finger is)
what's right about the g. o. world

what's wrong with(between me and we)
    the g--d -ld w. isn't that it
can't exist(and is that the
    g. o. w. is full of)delete

most(people

simply

can't)
won't(most
parent people mustn't

shouldn't)most daren't

(sortof people well
youknow kindof)
aint

&

even
(not having
most ever lived

people always)don't

die(becoming most
buried unbecomingly
very

by

most)people

kumrads die because they're told)
kumrads die before they're old
(kumrads aren't afraid to die
kumrads don't
and kumrads won't
believe in life)and death know whie

(all good kumrads you can tell
by their altruistic smell
moscow pipes good kumrads dance)
kumrads enjoy
s.freud knows whoy
the hope that you may mess your pance

every kumrad is a bit
of quite unmitigated hate
(travelling in a futile groove
god knows why)
and so do i
(because they are afraid to love

does yesterday's perfection seem not quite

so clever as the pratfall of a clown
(should stink of failure more than wars of feet

all things whose slendering sweetness touched renown)
suddenly themselves if all dreams unmake
(when in a most smashed unworld stands unslain

he which knows not if any anguish struck
how thin a ghost so deep and he might live)
yes,partly nor some edgeless star could give
that anguish room;but likes it only this

eternal mere one bursting soul
                              why,then

comes peace unto men who are always men
while a man shall which a god sometimes is

I the lost shoulders S the empty spine

numb(and
that was
and that
was cling)

on
win
ter
sc

ribbled
lonely truth(from
hang
from droop

w
ar
pin
g dre

ams
whichful sarcasms
papery deathfuls)awaits
yes

this alive secretly i
frantic this serene
mightily how rooted
who of iron

emptied.hills.listen.
,not,alive,trees,dream(
ev:ery:wheres:ex:tend:ing:hush

)
 andDark
IshbusY
ing-roundly-dis

tinct;chuck
lings,laced
ar:e.by(

fleet&panelike&frailties
!throughwhich!brittlest!whitewhom!
f
   l o a t?)
            r
              h y t h m s

snow)says!Says
over un
      graves
           der,speaking
(says.word
Less)ly(goes

folds?folds)cold
stones(o-l-d)names
aren'ts

)L
  iv
es(c
    omeS

says)s;n;o;w(says

W
I

elds)
un
  forgetting
        un.
der(theys)the

:se!crumbs things?Its
noyesiyou
he-she
(Weres

how dark and single,where he ends,the earth
(whose texture feels of pride and loneliness
alive like some dream giving more than all
life's busy little dyings may possess)

how sincere large distinct and natural
he comes to his disappearance;as a mind
full without fear might faithfully lie down
to so much sleep they only understand

enormously which fail—look:with what ease
that bright how plural tide measures her guest
(as critics will upon a poet feast)

meanwhile this ghost goes under,his drowned girth
are mountains;and beyond all hurt of praise
the unimaginable night not known

into a truly
curving form
enters my
soul

feels all small
facts dissolved
by the lewd guess
of fabulous immensity

the sky screamed
the sun died)
the ship lifts
on seas of iron

breathing heights eating
steepness the
ship climbs
murmuring silver mountains

which
disappear(and
only
was night

and through only this night a
mightily form moves
whose passenger and whose
pilot my spirit is

conceive a man,should he have anything
would give a little more than it away

(his autumn's winter being summer's spring
who moved by standing in november's may)
from whose(if loud most howish time derange

the silent whys of such a deathlessness)
remembrance might no patient mind unstrange
learn(nor could all earth's rotting scholars guess
that life shall not for living find the rule)

and dark beginnings are his luminous ends
who far less lonely than a fire is cool
took bedfellows for moons,mountains for friends

—open your thighs to fate and(if you can
withholding nothing)World,conceive a man

```
SNOW

cru
   is
      ingw Hi
sperf
      ul
lydesc

BYS FLUTTERFULLY IF

(endbegi ndesginb ecend)tang
lesp
     ang
le
  s
    ofC omeg o

CRINGE WITHS

lilt(
     -ing-
          lyful
of)!
    (s
r

BIRDS BECAUSE AGAINS

emarkable
          s)h?
              y& a
                  (from n
o(into whe)re f
              ind)
nd
   ArE

GLIB SCARCELYEST AMONGS FLOWERING
```

```
move
de-ply,rain
(dream hugely)wish
firmly.   splendidly advancing colour

strike
into form
(actually)realness
kill

(make
strangely)known(establish
new)come,what
Being!open us open

our
selves.  create
(suddenly announce:hurl)
blind full steep love
```

as if as

if a mys
teriouSly("i am alive"

)
 brave

ly and(th
e moon's al-down)most whis
per(here)ingc r O

wing;ly:cry.be,gi N s agAins

t b
ecomin
gsky?t r e e s
!

m ore&(o uto f)mor e torn(f og r

e
elingwhiRls)are pouring rush fields drea
mf(ull
      y
         are.)
&
som

ewhereishbudofshape

now,s
tI
r
ghost

?s

tirf lic;k
e rsM-o
:ke(c.
      l

i,

m
 !
b
)& it:s;elf,

mmamakmakemakesWwOwoRworLworlD

here's to opening and upward,to leaf and to sap
and to your(in my arms flowering so new)
self whose eyes smell of the sound of rain

and here's to silent certainly mountains;and to
a disappearing poet of always,snow
and to morning;and to morning's beautiful friend
twilight(and a first dream called ocean)and

let must or if be damned with whomever's afraid
down with ought with because with every brain
which thinks it thinks,nor dares to feel(but up
with joy:and up with laughing and drunkenness)

here's to one undiscoverable guess
of whose mad skill each world of blood is made
(whose fatal songs are moving in the moon

out of a supermetamathical subpreincestures
pooped universe(of croons canned
à la vallee and preserved goldfishian gestures)
suddenly sally rand

handsomely who did because she could what the movies try
to do because they can't i mean move
yes sir she jes was which the radio aint(proov
-ing that the quickness of the fand intrigues the fly)

for know all men(χαίρετε)
as it was in the beginning it(rejoice)
was and ever shall be nor every partialness beats one entirety
neither may shadow down flesh neither may vibration create voice

if therefore among foul pains appears an if emerges a joy let
's thank indecent
god p.s. the most successful b.o.fully speaking concession at the recent
world's fair was the paytoilet

theys s0 alive
               (who is
                    ?niggers)

          Not jes
          livin
        not Jes alive But
      So alive(they

    s
    born alive)
     some folks aint born
    somes born dead an
   somes born alive(but

   niggers
  is
 all
 born
so
Alive)

      ump-A-tum
         ;tee-die

       uM-tuM
          tidl
            -id

          umptyumpty(00——

                                  !
         ting
     Bam-
   :do)
,chippity.

the boys i mean are not refined
they go with girls who buck and bite
they do not give a fuck for luck
they hump them thirteen times a night

one hangs a hat upon her tit
one carves a cross in her behind
they do not give a shit for wit
the boys i mean are not refined

they come with girls who bite and buck
who cannot read and cannot write
who laugh like they would fall apart
and masturbate with dynamite

the boys i mean are not refined
they cannot chat of that and this
they do not give a fart for art
they kill like you would take a piss

they speak whatever's on their mind
they do whatever's in their pants
the boys i mean are not refined
they shake the mountains when they dance

sometimes
            in)Spring a someone will lie(glued
among familiar things newly which are
transferred with dusk)wondering why this star
does not fall into his mind
                        feeling
throughout ignorant disappearing me
hurling vastness of love(sometimes in Spring
somewhere between what is and what may be
unknown most secret i will breathe such crude
perfection as divides by timelessness
that heartbeat)
            mightily forgetting all
which will forget him(emptying our soul
of emptiness)priming at every pore
a deathless life with magic until peace
outthunders silence.
                    And(night climbs the air

swi(
   across!gold's

rouNdly
)ftblac
kl(ness)y

a-motion-upo-nmotio-n

Less?
   thE
(against
is
)Swi

mming

(w-a)s
bIr

d,

ondumonde"

   (first than caref
  ully;pois
edN-o wt he
n
,whysprig
      sli

nkil
 -Y-
  strol(pre)ling(cise)dy(ly)na(
  mite)

  :yearnswoons;

  &Isdensekil-
  ling-whipAlert-floatScor
  ruptingly)

       ça-y-est
       droppe5
        qu'est-ce que tu veux
        Dwrith
         il est trop fort le nègre
        esn7othingish8s
       c'est fini
      pRaW,1T;O:
      allons
    9
     &
    .

       (musically-who?

  pivoting)
  SmileS

   "ah1brhoon

```
floatfloafloflf
lloloa
tatoatloatf loat fl oat
f loatI ngL


y


&fris
klispin
glyT
     w
       irlErec


,


t,
;d
;:a:
nC.eda:Nci;ddaanncciinn


(GlY)


a
 nda
     n-saint
dance!Dan
Sai ntd anc


&e&


—cupidoergosum
spun=flash
omiepsicronlonO—
megaeta?
          p
           aul D-as-in-tip-toe r


apeR
```

silent unday by silently not night

did the great world(in darkly taking rain)
drown,beyond sound
                        down(slowly
                                    beneath
                                                sight
fall
      ing)fall
                ing through touch
                                    less stillness(seized

among what ghostly nevers of again)
silent not night by silently unday
life's bright less dwindled to a leastful most
under imagination. When(out of sheer

nothing)came a huger than fear a

white with madness wind and broke oceans and tore
mountains from their sockets and strewed the black air
with writhing alive skies—and in death's place
new fragrantly young earth space opening was.
Were your eyes:lost,believing;hushed with when

much i cannot)
tear up the world:& toss
it away;or
cause one causeless cloud to purely grow

but,never
doubt my weakness
makes more than most
strength(less than these how

less than least flowers of rain)thickly
i fail slenderly i
win(like touch all stars or
to live in the moon

a while)and shall
carve time so we'll before
what's death
come(in one bed.

at dusk
        just when
the Light is filled with birds
seriously
i begin

to climb the best hill,
driven by black wine.
a village does not move behind
my eye

the windmills are
silent
their flattened arms
complain steadily against the west

one Clock dimly cries
nine,i stride among the vines
(my heart pursues
against the little moon

a here and there lark
                    who;rises,
and;droops
as if upon a thread invisible)

A graveyard dreams through its
cluttered and brittle emblems,or
a field(and i pause among
the smell of minute mown lives)oh

my spirit you
tumble
climb
        and mightily fatally

i remark how through deep lifted
fields Oxen distinctly move,a
yellowandbluish cat(perched why
Curvingly at this)window;yes

women sturdily meander in my
mind,woven by always upon
sunset,
crickets within me whisper

whose erect blood finally
trembles,emerging to perceive
buried in cliff
                precisely

at the Ending of this road,
a candle in a shrine:
its puniest flame persists
shaken by the sea

Spring(side

walks are)is
most(windows where blaze

naLOVEme
crazily
ships

bulge hearts by
darts pierced lazily writhe
lurch faceflowers stutter
treebodies wobbly-

ing thing
-birds)sing-
u
(cities are houses
people are flies who

buzz on)-lar(windows called sidewalks
of houses called cities)spring
most singular-
ly(cities are houses are)is(are owned

by a m- by
a -n by a
-oo-

is old as
the jews are a moon is

as round as)Death

what a proud dreamhorse pulling(smoothloomingly)through
(stepp)this(ing)crazily seething of this
raving city screamingly street wonderful

flowers And o the Light thrown by Them opens

sharp holes in dark places paints eyes touches hands with new-
ness and these startled whats are a(piercing clothes thoughts kiss
-ing wishes bodies)squirm-of-frightened shy are whichs small
its hungry for Is for Love Spring thirsty for happens
only and beautiful
                        there is a ragged beside the who limps
man crying silence upward
                            —to have tasted Beautiful to have known
Only to have smelled Happens—skip dance kids hop point at
red blue yellow violet white orange green-
ness

        o what a proud dreamhorse moving(whose feet
almost walk air). now who stops. Smiles.he
                                stamps

Jehovah buried,Satan dead,
do fearers worship Much and Quick;
badness not being felt as bad,
itself thinks goodness what is meek;
obey says toc,submit says tic,
Eternity's a Five Year Plan:
if Joy with Pain shall hang in hock
who dares to call himself a man?

go dreamless knaves on Shadows fed,
your Harry's Tom,your Tom is Dick;
while Gadgets murder squawk and add,
the cult of Same is all the chic;
by instruments,both span and spic,
are justly measured Spic and Span:
to kiss the mike is Jew turn kike
who dares to call himself a man?

loudly for Truth have liars pled,
their heels for Freedom slaves will click;
where Boobs are holy,poets mad,
illustrious punks of Progress shriek;
when Souls are outlawed,Hearts are sick,
Hearts being sick,Minds nothing can:
if Hate's a game and Love's a fuck
who dares to call himself a man?

King Christ,this world is all aleak;
and lifepreservers there are none:
and waves which only He may walk
Who dares to call Himself a man.

worshipping Same
they squirm and they spawn
and a world is for them,them;whose
death's to be born)

his birth is their fear is their blind fear
—haunts all unsleep
this cry of one fiend,
a thousand dreams thick

(cringing they brood
breeding they wince)
his laugh is a million griefs wide(it
shall bury much stench)

and a hundred joys high are such shoulders
as cowards will scheme
to harness:let all
unfools of unbeing

set traps for his heart,
lay snares for his feet
(who wanders through only white darkness
who moves in black light

dancing isn'ts on why,digging bridges with mirrors
from whispers to stars;
climbing silence for ifs
diving under because)

only who'll say
"and this be my fame,
the harder the wind blows the
taller i am"

this mind made war
being generous
this heart could dare)
unhearts can less

unminds must fear
because and why
what filth is here
unlives do cry

on him they shat
they shat encore
he laughed and spat
(this life could dare

freely to give
as gives a friend
not those who slave
unselves to lend

for hope of hope
must coo or boo
may strut or creep
ungenerous who

ape deftly aims
they dare not share)
such make their names
(this poet made war

whose naught and all
sun are and moon
come fair come foul
he goes alone

daring to dare
for joy of joy)
what stink is here
unpoets do cry

unfools unfree
undeaths who live
nor shall they be
and must they have

at him they fart
they fart full oft
(with mind with heart
he spat and laughed

with self with life
this poet arose
nor hate nor grief
can go where goes

this whyless soul
a loneliest road
who dares to stroll
almost this god

this surely dream
perhaps this ghost)
humbly and whom
for worst or best

(and proudly things
only which grow
and the rain's wings
the birds of snow

things without name
beyond because
things over blame
things under praise

glad things or free
truly which live
always shall be
may never have)

do i salute
(by moon by sun
i deeply greet
this fool and man

when
    from a sidewalk
                  out of(blown never quite to
-gether by large sorry)creatures out
of(clumsily shining out of)instru-
ments,waltzing;undigestibly:groans.bounce

!o-ras-ourh an-dorg-an ble-at-ssw-ee-t-noth ings orarancidhurd
ygurdygur glingth umpssomet hings(whi,le sp,arrow,s wince
among those skeletons of these trees)
                               when
                                    sunbeams loot
furnished rooms through whose foul windows absurd
clouds cruise nobly ridiculous skies

(the;mselve;s a;nd scr;a;tch-ing lousy full.of.rain
beggars yaw:nstretchy:awn)
                    then,
                        o my love
                              ,then
it's Spring
        immortal Always & lewd shy New

and upon the beyond imagining spasm rise
we
    you-with-me
                around(me)you
                      IYou

love is a place
& through this place of
love move
(with brightness of peace)
all places

yes is a world
& in this world of
yes live
(skilfully curled)
all worlds

sh estiffl
ystrut sal
lif san
dbut sth

epoutin(gWh.ono:w
s li psh ergo
wnd ow n,
            r
Eve

aling 2 a
-sprout eyelands)sin
uously&them&twi
tching,begins

unununun?
butbutbut??
tonton???
ing????

—Out-&
        steps;which
flipchucking
.grIns
gRiNdS

d is app ea r in gly
eyes grip live loop croon mime
nakedly hurl asquirm the
dip&giveswoop&swoon&ingly

seethe firm swirl hips whirling climb to
GIVE
(yoursmine mineyours yoursmine
!
i()t)

```
(b
  eL1
     s?
       bE


-ginningly)come-swarm:faces
ar;rive go.faces a(live)
sob bel
ls


(pour wo
        (things)
               men
                    selves-them


inghurl)bangbells(yawnchurches
suck people)reel(dark-
ly)whirling
in


(b
  ellSB
       el
          Ls)


-to sun(crash).Streets
glit
ter
a,strut:do;colours;are:m,ove


o im
    -pos-
        sibl
              y


(ShoutflowereD
flowerish boom
b el Lsb El l
s!cry)


(be
   llsbe
       lls)
            b
              (be
                llsbell)
                      ells
                           (sbells)
```

love's function is to fabricate unknownness

(known being wishless;but love,all of wishing)
though life's lived wrongsideout,sameness chokes oneness
truth is confused with fact,fish boast of fishing

and men are caught by worms(love may not care
if time totters,light droops,all measures bend
nor marvel if a thought should weigh a star
—dreads dying least;and less,that death should end)

how lucky lovers are(whose selves abide
under whatever shall discovered be)
whose ignorant each breathing dares to hide
more than most fabulous wisdom fears to see

(who laugh and cry)who dream,create and kill
while the whole moves;and every part stands still:

we)under)over,the thing of floating Of
;elate
shyly a-live keen parallel specks float-ing create
height,
       liv-

ing
   ly who:seemSwoop
             (whir
-ling be,yond!thought
are.more(Than girl

's
tears boy Dream's)forge

tful:e
     ver than,is e
                ven:th
                    e(s
                      e
                        a's;m
                           e,
                             m(or.y

```
    birds(
          here,inven
    ting air
    U
    )sing

    tw
    iligH(
    t's
         v
           va
             vas
    vast

    ness.Be)look
    now
        (come
    soul;
    &:and

who
     s)e
          voi
c
es
(
 are
      ar
        a
```

Do.
omful
relaxing

-ly)i
downrise outwrithein-
ing upfall and

Am the glad deep the living from nowh
-ere(!firm!)exp-
anding,am a fe

-rvently(susta-
inin
-gness Am

root air rock day)
:you;
smile,hands

(an-
onymo
-Us

if night's mostness(and whom did merely day
close)
     opens
        if more than silence silent are more
flowering than stars whitely births of mind

if air is throbbing prayers whom kneeling eyes
(until perfectly their imperfect gaze
climbs this steep fragrance of eternity)
world by than worlds immenser world will pray

so(unlove disappearing)only your
less than guessed more than beauty begins the
most not imagined life adventuring
who would feel if spring's least breathing should cause
a colour
     and i do not know him
            (and

while behind death's death whenless voices sing
everywhere your selves himself recognize)

death(having lost)put on his universe
and yawned:it looks like rain
(they've played for timelessness
with chips of when)
that's yours;i guess
you'll have to loan me pain
to take the hearse,
see you again.

Love(having found)wound up such pretty toys
as themselves could not know:
the earth tinily whirls;
while daisies grow
(and boys and girls
have whispered thus and so)
and girls with boys
to bed will go,

come(all you mischief-
hatchers hatch
mischief)all you

guilty
   scamper(you bastards throw dynamite)
     let knowings magic
   with bright credos each divisible fool

   (life imitate gossip fear unlife
mean
 -ness,and
   to succeed in not
     dying)

   Is will still occur;birds disappear
  becomingly:a thunderbolt compose poems
not because harm symmetry
 earthquakes starfish(but
   because nobody
     can sell the Moon to The)moon

be of love(a little)
More careful
Than of everything
guard her perhaps only

A trifle less
(merely beyond how very)
closely than
Nothing,remember love by frequent

anguish(imagine
Her least never with most
memory)give entirely each
Forever its freedom

(Dare until a flower,
understanding sizelessly sunlight
Open what thousandth why and
discover laughing)

reason let others give and realness bring—
ask the always impossible of me
and shall who wave among your deepening
thighs a greedier wand than even death's

what beneath breathing selves transported are
into how suddenly so huge a home
(only more than immeasurable dream
wherelessly spiralling)beyond time's sky

and through this opening universe will wraiths
of doom rush(which all ghosts of life became)
and does our fatally unshadowing fate
put on one not imaginable star

:then a small million of dark voices sing
against the awful mystery of light

brIght

bRight s??? big
(soft)

soft near calm
(Bright)
calm st?? holy

(soft briGht deep)
yeS near sta? calm star big yEs
alone
(wHo

Yes
near deep whO big alone soft near
deep calm deep
????Ht ?????T)
Who(holy alone)holy(alone holy)alone

morsel miraculous and meaningless

secret on luminous whose selves and lives
imperishably feast all timeless souls

(the not whose spiral hunger may appease
what merely riches of our pretty world
sweetly who flourishes,swiftly which fails

but out of serene perfectly Nothing hurled
into young New entirely arrives
gesture past fragrance fragrant;a than pure

more signalling of singular most flame
and surely poets only understands)
honour this loneliness of even him

who fears and eyes lifts lifting hopes and hands
—nourish my failure with thy freedom:star

isful beckoningly fabulous crumb

AND
THANKS
TO
R.H.C.

AFTERWORD

by

George James Firmage

The earliest known version of E. E. Cummings's sixth "bookofpoems"—an untitled manuscript containing fifty of the seventy-one poems published in the collection—was sent to the John Simon Guggenheim Foundation in February 1934 as Cumming's report of his activity while holding a fellowship the previous year. The manuscript remained buried in the foundation's files until Professor Richard S. Kennedy uncovered it in the Guggenheim's offices in 1977. Seventeen of the poems in this manuscript are textually or typographically different from the versions eventually published.

The only other surviving manuscript of Cummings's 1935 collection—a rearrangement with additions of an earlier sixty-nine-poem version—is now in the Clifton Waller Barrett Library of the University of Virginia.[1] This is the version that was typeset and published by the Golden Eagle Press on April 15, 1935.

In addition to the manuscript, the Virginia collection also includes the original "First Lines" index of sixty-nine poems, the "Revised Index" to the seventy-one-poem version, two pages of the poet's designs for the layout of the book, and a short letter from his agent, Bernice Baumgarten of Brandt & Brandt, listing the fourteen "simple-minded people [publishers] who refused the new collection...." The latter was clearly Cummings's inspiration for the title and initial dedication of the published volume. The terminal dedication to his mother, "R[ebecca] H[aswell] C[ummings]," who paid for the printing of *No Thanks,* is penciled in Cummings's hand on the back of the letter.

The first printing of *No Thanks*[2] was unusual in that the texts of the poems were imposed parallel to the spine instead of perpendicular to it. This permitted the longest of the poems—numbers 4 and 60 in the current edition—to start at the top of a two-page spread and continue without interruption across the gutter of the book to the bottom, facing page. However, in order to do this, it became necessary to change the manuscript order of poems 4 and 5 and 59 and 60.

The present "Typescript Edition" of *No Thanks* is the first complete version of the poet's final manuscript to be published in its original order and the only separate printing of the book since its initial appearance forty-four years ago. The typography of the poems, which, as Cummings himself noted, cannot be "retranslate[d]...out of typewriter language into linotype-ese," follows the final manuscript exactly, as do the texts of all the poems except numbers 11 and 63. The latter, which are stylistically inconsistent in their use of the parenthesis, have been corrected against earlier manuscript versions in the Houghton Library, Harvard University.[3]

Notes

[1] Deposit 6246-a.

[2] *No Thanks* was available–in three different editions: a signed "holograph edition" of 9 copies with the text of poem 44 (the then too-explicit "the boys i mean are not refined") in Cummings's hand; and a signed "deluxe edition" of 90 copies, and an unsigned "first trade edition" of 900 copies without poem 44.

[3] bMS Am1823.5 (70), "ci-gît 1 Foetus(unborn not to die," and bMS Am1823.5 (54), "birds(/here,inven."